MOUNTAINS

EMPOWERMENT THROUGH EDUCATION

MAX R. JEAN-PAUL, Ed.D.

The content of this book is of the author and does not reflect the views, official policy, or position of the Department of Education. This book is to provide information and inspiration.

Cover Design by Burconur

ISBN 13: 978-0-578-88247-5
Library of Congress Control Number: 2021906034

Citadelle Publishing LLC
www.Citadellebooks.com

CITADELLE
PUBLISHING

This book is dedicated to my family, parents, siblings and late grandmother. To my wife, thanks (merci) for being my rock. I could not have done this without you. To all the students and staff I had the privilege to work with.

CONTENTS

	Forward	vii
	Preface	ix
Chapter 1	Foundation	1
Chapter 2	Transforming the Perception	11
Chapter 3	Teaching	25
Chapter 4	Leadership	33
Chapter 5	Principal	41
Chapter 6	Lessons Learned	63
Chapter 7	Conclusion	77
	Acknowledgments	81
	About The Author	83

FORWARD

To be Haitian in the 1980s was to be forged in fire. The narrative of Haitians that many in the United States of America promoted was one of deficiency, diminishment, and denial. Fortunately, for those children and adolescents whose parents and caregivers understood the power of identity, they were able to be exposed to a different experience.

Dr. Jean-Paul is an example of what overcoming obstacles, navigating barriers, and forging a powerful life purpose looks like when we embrace the truth of Haiti and the power of the Haitian story. Coming of age in Brooklyn, NY, avoiding the pitfalls that ensnared many young Black men in the '80s and early 90s, and achieving significant heights in public service is what embodies this Haitian educator and his success story.

This story is more than a biography, it is a life map and a blueprint of immigrants pursuing their dream, a set of plans for people of color defying the deficit-based narratives, and an inspiration to educators who want to remember why education matters.

Rubain J. Dorancy, Esq. MPA
TRIAD Consulting Strategies

PREFACE

As a black man, I always felt like I was climbing a mountain. Life gave me obstacles that I had to surmount daily. My atmosphere growing up in Brooklyn New York, with the racism and bias, were like the rugged terrains of Bonnet à l'Evêque that my ancestors had to climb to create the beautiful Citadelle.

In this book, I will describe my family, culture, values, and their influences on my life; the tough decisions and struggles I had to make and their long-term impacts on me. I hope you find a connection with my experience and stay determined with whatever you are working through. Take the immediate action you need for yourself.

As an educator, I have taught and mentored many students, teachers, and aspiring administrators. It brings me joy to see what my students have become and continue to aspire to. I have worked with many educators across the country and internationally; I am very thankful to them for always welcoming my voice. I firmly believe that relationships make a difference in teaching and learning. The collection of student voices, teacher voices, and community voices empower me to want to do more.

As a youth from Brooklyn, I never thought I would impact others or know that others would want to hear from me. I am deeply honored and humbled. My first visit to Haiti also impacted me in multiple ways. I learned to appreciate life and how to deal with it while understanding that there are matters that are beyond my control.

The book is divided into chapters that describe

- My background
- My first time in Haiti and its impact on me
- My role as a teacher
- My role as a school administrator
- My school community
- My Community involvement

Each chapter is attached with a proverb that represents my culture. In Haitian Creole, a proverb is used to emphasize a point as a universal fact or satirical response. After conversing with my family and elders, I would conduct my research to understand what was being messaged to me.

As you read through this book, you will see and understand my professional growth. I continue to read, reflect, and learn new strategies to move my school community. Despite systemic disparities and indecipherable images of inner-city youth, I am proud of my students, teachers, and community. They understand and value education. I am proud of the students' outcomes and teachers' success over the years. This would not have been possible without trusting relationships and conversations with solutions.

Understanding the data and other challenges is essential.

I am truly humbled and pleased to share my experiences with you. In my role as a school leader, I enjoy meeting with young people, students, and educators from around the world. I enjoy waking up every morning to go to work. The handshakes, smiles, and conversations are priceless. Supporting our learners is a priority. Making sure their mental health and instructional needs are met is critical.

The resiliency I witnessed from my grandmother, parents, and students is powerful. The willingness to learn a new language, skills, and passion to climb demonstrates the power of education. I will continue to work with my family, students, and everyone around me. I am profoundly happy to create this opportunity for you to share my journey.

1

FOUNDATION

"Knowledge is power, community is strength, & positive attitude is everything" – L. Armstrong

Growing up in a Haitian household in Brooklyn was amusing, tremendous in learning, comical, strict, and a discovery of an unknown world of Haiti. The Haitian culture is rich with history, tales, hard-work, mountains, cuisines, education, and characters. My grandmother, parents, and relatives spoke Haitian Creole. My sister and I were the only ones born in the United States of America. I was born and raised in Brooklyn. I lived on Bushwick Avenue.

The neighborhood was surrounded by the J and L train line. The local buses were the B52, B26, B60, and B24 that operated on Broadway Avenue. The neighborhood was predominantly African-American and Puerto Rican with a small percentage of West Indian descendants and Central Americans. There were a variety of Brownstones, cars, and other types of houses in the neighborhood. So much has changed since the 1980s and 90s. I learned years later that my old house was the gateway for many families and friends that came to the United States of America.

My mother is from Les Cayes, Haiti. She grew up in Port Salut, a small suburb of Les Cayes with cobblestone roads, palm trees and beautiful beaches. She is soft-spoken and loves to dance. My father is from Pétion-Ville, a suburb outside of Port-Au-Prince. He came to the United States of America in his teens. My parents married and had my sister and I. They both believed in symbolism, history, and the American dream. My father was an electrical engineer and my mother worked as an administrative assistant in a bank. They always prepared us for the precipice of life and beyond.

I am very thankful to my mother for always taking the time to broaden my palette and teach me how to cook and bake. These are some of my most memorable moments. I would walk to the Gates Avenue station and take the J train to meet her at our destination. She introduced me to various cuisines from other cultures such as Malaysian, Indian, and Chinese. She would find different restaurants for us to explore. I was always excited and ready for this new adventure. It was something different from the traditional food I ate. We would discuss the food's texture and current events. She would say, "Son, kisa ou panse?" (Son, what do you think?) I would respond with my feelings and thoughts about the food. I appreciated hearing her laughter and perspectives on outcomes.

My father was a militant, funny, candid, and proud man. He always pushed me to assert myself, my existence, and my identity. Society was not to define who I became. Every book I read, report I wrote, and historical film I watched had a lesson behind it. He kept it simple and straight to the point. We would have endless conversations about race, current events, Haiti, American politics, social injustice, and sports. Reflecting on these conversations, I remember why it was important to create my narrative and not let society create it for me. His civics lessons were critical and the inequities he faced then are still present today. He always broke topics down and reminded me of the impending crisis affecting people of color globally. Besides that, he reinforced daily the importance of education as a pillar to whatever I decide to accomplish.

My mornings would start off with talking with my grandmother over a cup of coffee. She would tell me stories about her life in Haiti and how it changed when she came to the United States of America. Most of the time, she spoke to me in Haitian Creole and I responded in my broken Haitian Creole. She would correct me and move on. I remember her telling me how the roosters would wake her up. Now she depended on the alarm clock, cars driving by, and the sounds of the J train. She would leave the house at 7 am to catch the 7:15 am train to Manhattan. She would be back by 3 pm to cook dinner for the entire family. She loved to cook. Every day, we had rice, boiled plantain, and some type of meat. If the rice did not have beans, there was a bean soup (sòs pwa) to complement it. We had a schedule

Monday: leftovers or spaghetti (as I got older, I found out that Haitians like to eat spaghetti for breakfast!)
Tuesday: white rice with a type of bean soup and a type of meat
Wednesday: surprise (there was no rice)
Thursday: rice and beans with legumes (coyote)
Friday: white rice with a type of bean soup with fish
Saturday: fried plantain with pork (griot) or turkey or "Fritay night."
Sunday: rice and beans, chicken, macaroni au gratin, salad.

All family members assisted with the cooking. At the dinner table, I would listen to their dreams, aspirations and challenges of starting over by going to school and learning English. At a young age, I started to fathom resiliency. For someone to leave their country, friends and culture, to learn a new system is commendable. My grandmother, parents, and relatives did it. Their narratives compelled me to want to do more with my life and not settle for less. The expectations were high. I loved learning about the different proverbs and their message. I always wondered when I would visit Haiti. For some people of my family, coming to the United States of America was a choice, but for others, it was not. I will share more on this in a later chapter. Striving for a good education was non-negotiable in my household. As a result, some family members became teachers, engineers, doctors, and lawyers.

My grandmother would tell me to work and study hard. She would use herself as an example of perseverance and tenacity. She left her country and family to seek a better opportunity. She learned English, saved money and was able to purchase a house and bring her children over to join her. I would ask her the following questions:

How did she adapt and adjust to this new environment?

Was it difficult to learn English?

What was it like to wear extra clothing in the Fall and Winter being from a Caribbean island?

As a youth, I had so many questions. Her detailed stories left an impression on me. I always found that to be remarkable. I enjoyed our many conversations and her words of wisdom.

The implications of Haiti and misconceptions were always corrected. Positive vibes always remained at home. My family was very proud and made sure I knew that Haitians lead the first successful slavery revolution and other advances. Later in the book, I will go into the deep-rooted practices that were a norm in my household to understand my culture and identity. Some of the misconceptions and hardships will be addressed as I dive deeper into my upbringing and leadership approaches.

First Misconception

During the 80's, the Centers for Disease Control put out a report about Haitians being the hosts of HIV/AIDS. You can imagine what my dinner table conversations were like around that time. My family was upset and in a rage. They took part in the marches to denounce this false publication. I remember listening to the radio shows that were in English and Haitian Creole on that topic. I was instructed that the information was false and not to believe what anybody tells you. At that time, I started questioning the validity of science and government policies. In school, the topic never came up. However, I was ready to dispute what anyone had to say on the subject. Wait until I share my High School years with you.

Second Misconception

Also, in my earlier youth, the Crack Era was at its peak. Empty (crack) houses were everywhere and crack vials littered the streets. I remember the "Say no to Drugs" campaign and my parents always telling me to do the same. My sister and I would walk to school and back home, witnessing the ills of poverty.

I remember the story of David Aupont, the young man who said no to drugs and was set on fire in the streets of Brooklyn. David was an immigrant from Haiti. He was picked on and refused to try drugs. He would rather get burned than take the drugs. He said, "my family does not take drugs." I was so proud of him for taking a stand and not being afraid. In addition, he represented his identity and demonstrated perseverance. I thought of all the misconceptions that people had about immigrants. The media always portrayed poverty, thick accents, torn clothing, boats, and sickness. I started to wonder how my grandmother, parents, and family dealt with this daily negative imagery. In my household, I was told of beautiful homes, beaches, weather, and resiliency. My family kept me grounded and protected. I was always reminded of the beauty of Haiti.

Adolescent Years

I would continue to wake up early and have coffee with my parents. We would discuss current events, school, and life in Haiti. I had to take three trains to get to High School every day. I would have to be in school by 8 am for first period. If the weapon scanning lines were too long, I would miss first period, go purchase a bacon, egg, and cheese sandwich with juice, go congregate with my friends and chat about music, sports, and events.

Clara Barton High School had a diversity of students from the Caribbean. However, the stigma of being Haitian was prevalent back then. I would tell other students to leave the Haitian students alone. They would say, "Max, I did not know you were

Haitian". I would respond and say, "Yes". The common saying was, "Yo, you don't dress or look like them". I would follow up with "What do Haitians look like?" These common stereotypes were frustrating, draining, and daunting.

As a youth growing up, I enjoyed playing sports, listening to hip hop music, and reading. I would get into discussions with my family about the hip-hop culture and its positive messages. They would introduce me to some of the traditional Haitian music and other musicians like "Fela Kuti". My aunt took me to my first concert, "Krush Groove". I had to write a paper for my father comparing and contrasting the different genres. As a result, I have an appreciation for all types of music.

I would sit on the stoop, outside of my house, with my neighborhood friends. We would play dominos, spades, and various card games. We also discussed the top five sports figures, music artists, and songs. Sometimes, it would get so loud that my grandmother and parents would come outside to see if everything was okay. They would then join the conversation and give their input.

Finally, I never thought I would see the age of twenty-five. One late summer, I was sitting in my backyard and saw fire crackers. I later realized that I actually saw small flashes and the sounds were gun shots. The amount of shootings and robberies that took place around me was scary. The harassment from law enforcement and implicit biases towards me for being a black male was not easy. It was difficult to sleep at night at times, but this was my reality. In addition to hearing stories about "The Central Park 5" and the murder of Yusef Hawkins, I witnessed two homicides that forever changed my life. I was unable to sleep. I learned to be more aware of my surroundings and how life can easily be taken away. As a youth, witnessing trauma and dealing with it was not easy. In Haitian Creole, we say, "Jé wè, bouch pé" (eyes see, mouth stays shut). In other words, "no snitching". Having sleepless nights and lack of focus was hard. I was scared to walk the streets. The causes of crime were already evident in my community with drugs and poverty. Seeing crack vials, prostitution, alcoholics, abandoned buildings and empty lots was a norm for me. Whether I was walking to school, the supermarket, or the bodega, this was my environment. Over time, I learned to manage my anxiety and found safety in reading my books and writing. I started to volunteer and got involved in school clubs. As an adult, I understood trauma. My family understood some of my struggles as a young black male but would not succumb to accepting the American ways of justice. They would nourish me with reading materials and history on how to overcome these hurdles.

I would escape the daily dilemmas by going to the libraries and learning more about the world. I had a choice to walk to the library on Irving Street or Bushwick Avenue. As a young man, I thought it was cool.

Haitian Proverb:

Men anpil chay pa lou.

Many hands make the load lighter

2

TRANSFORMING
THE PERCEPTION

"Dr. Max Jean-Paul is a family man who has a passion to make his community better. His love for his students is immediately reflected in the first few minutes of a conversation with him. Max is on a mission to make this world a better place for our youth, especially our black and brown youth." - Aisha Demosthenes, M. S., CCC-SLP, Co-founder of Moms Who Care, Inc.

Obstacles

Education was always emphasized in my household. My father required my sister and I to read books every week besides our school requirements. After reading, we had to write a one-page summary. He would tutor Mathematics and English to all the students on the block and also assist newly arrived students from everywhere. He stressed the importance of knowledge, liberation and pan-Africanism. He would say, "no one can take away your brain. If I can come to this country and adapt, you can do it too." He always reminded us to reach for the stars and to not settle for less. He also retold us about our Haitian roots and taught us about the forefathers who set the path for many countries to achieve independence, including the United States of America. One book I had to read and remember was the "Black Jacobins" by C.L.R James. I was around twelve at that time. This book was about the Haitian Revolution and how Toussaint Louverture played a vital role in starting it. Toussaint was very smart, courageous, fearless, and determined for the freedom of slaves. I understood then that education and freedom are key to succeeding in life. I was also introduced to the author James Baldwin and enjoyed his use of words in dealing with racism in America.

I would complain about the social distractions around us and the circumstances like drugs, racism, shootings, and prostitution. My father would say, "poverty is a state of mind." One day, when I was 8 years old, my father drove me to someone's house and showed me a family of six living in a one-bedroom apartment. There I saw a young boy similar to my age working on his homework on his sleeping bag. My father looked at me and said, "Do you understand?" I replied, "Wi" (yes). I was quiet on my way back home. I know now that he was preparing me to deal with the emotions and struggles people face.

College Years

I was offered to attend several colleges and universities away from home. However, my parents promised me a vehicle and I decided to stay home and attend CUNY Brooklyn College. The day I graduated from High School was the same day I started my undergraduate studies.

By coincidence, my High School graduation ceremony was held at CUNY Brooklyn College. It was interesting to walk through a crowd of parents celebrating their child's success. The tears and pride of accomplishments were evident in both the students' and parents' faces. I had just lived that experience and was now ready to tackle the next chapter in my life. Earlier that day I was with my parents, dressed in a suit and taking pictures with friends. Time passes by so fast. I could not believe it.

As I entered the campus, there were vendors selling balloons and graduation items. I showed my identification and navigated my way to the building where my class was held. It felt different walking to class and not knowing anyone. There were all types of people from different backgrounds. I found my classroom and took a seat. The instructor introduced themselves and passed out a syllabus. Each pupil had to introduce themselves and the professor then proceeded with the class.

While in college, I had to work to pay for my tuition and car insurance. I took a variety of fine arts courses and other educational courses. I was involved in some of the academic clubs such as the National Black Science Students Organization and the Haitian American Students Organization. I also supported some of the political organizations on campus. In my spare time, I volunteered and taught GED\English at St. Jerome Catholic Church to recently arrived Haitian Immigrants. The elders in that class were very thankful and shared many stories with me after class.

First Time in Haiti

During one semester, I was offered the opportunity to study abroad in Haiti. This program involved diaspora from all around the world to take part in studying at Universitè Quisqueya. Students from Cuba, France, and other nations took part in this program. I was extremely excited and ready to see my parents' birthplace and revisit the stories my grandmother had shared with me. I had heard so much and now my dream was becoming a reality. Around this time, I had started working at the Arthur Ashe Institute for Public Health as a community coordinator. At the institute, I created a barbershop program called "Different Fades of Health".

My first visit to Haiti.

We selected barbershops in central Brooklyn to discuss public health issues that affected men of color such as prostate cancer, hypertension, and diabetes. Once a month, a health educator or clinician would speak to customers at various salons in Brooklyn. The sister program was called "Black Pearl".

I also worked with the late Dr. Rachel Fructher from SUNY Downstate. She was an epidemiologist and clinician. She encouraged me to do some research while I was visiting this great nation. I secured some donations for my trip to conduct two health fairs while I was in Haiti. I was successful in conducting one in Cap-Haitian and in the nation's capital, Port-au-Prince.

Haitian Merchants at Milot

I was amazed at the number of people who showed up for the event. At the fair, we conducted blood pressure and diabetes tests. The people were very thankful and humbled. Volunteers from local hospitals joined me in providing materials and screenings. I was overwhelmed by the number of people who came out to hear me speak.

Health Fair in Haiti

Despite the sweat on my forehead and my wet palms, I was ready to do this. My Haitian Creole was rusty but the crowd embraced me and thanked me for coming. In preparation for my trip to Haiti, I was able to form relationships with grass-root organizations that were conducting outstanding work in Haiti.

Health Fair Workshop in Haiti

Each health fair had over fifty people. I was very thankful to the Arthur Ashe Institute for Urban Health for sponsoring me.

When I arrived at Maïs-Gate Airport in Haiti, it was hot. The joy of landing in the first black independent nation and seeing some of the palm trees, mountains, fruits, and hearing Haitian Creole was breathtaking. It was everything my parents had shared with me as well as the books I read about Haiti. I took plenty of pictures and recorded some of the school's road trips. I was like a tourist in New York City, viewing the Statue of Liberty\Empire State Building in the busy streets of Manhattan.

Health Fair Workshop in Haiti

However, in class, the format was different from the United States. I was required to sit and listen to the professor lecture about the history of Haiti. Questions and discussions were limited. My classmates and I would later discuss the role of education in their respective countries. In the afternoon, I would walk to some of my relatives' homes and share my daily experiences with them.

They were just happy that I was in Haiti and getting a wonderful experience. I would also use the opportunity to practice speaking Haitian Creole. I was able to see the faces and hear the voices of the family members, in the portraits, lining the walls of my home in Brooklyn. I was happy that the dormitory was not too far. In the evening, I would write in my journal about my experience.

Visiting my family in Haiti was important for me. I got to see with my own eyes where my family was from. I sat with my elders and heard many stories from the past that I would someday share with my children. It was cool to hear stories about my great grandparents and grandmother. Seeing my family in person and not just speaking with them on the phone was different. Technology was not prevalent back then. There was no WhatsApp or Facetime, however, this was a memorable time in my life.

During my time in Haiti, visiting both the North and South of the island was fascinating. I gained a new perspective and more appreciation for this beautiful country. Taking the trip to the Citadelle la Ferrière in Milot was outstanding. The Citadelle is on the north coast and is referred to as the 7th or 8th wonder of the world, depending on what site you reference. In 1982 it was nominated as a UNESCO World Heritage Site.

It is a wonderful and fascinating place to visit. As you walk up the mountain, you can only imagine what it was like to carry materials and to help defend your country from the overseer.

Citadelle la Ferrière

When you arrive at the Citadelle, you can see the ocean and other forts. The people of the North take pride in the forefathers who lead Haiti to its independence. Two of the most notable were Toussaint Louverture and Jean-Jacques Dessalines.

As I walked around, I was thankful for the conversations and interactions with the elders, local merchants and street vendors (Machann).

My son climbing the Citadelle for the first time

Ayiti means "land of mountains," and the views are priceless. The food has many different cultures fused into great dishes that leave you wanting more. My favorite is white rice with green split peas (sòs pwa vèt), and meatballs (boulèt). There are dishes that are only native to Haitians, like black rice (diri ak djon djon) and fried goat (tassot). The various genres of music such as Kompa, Twoubadou, and Raboday originate from our Haiti. The temperature is tropical all year round. I was happy to visit the first free Black

Republic in the World. Many South American countries and others carry our bicolor on their flag as a symbol of respect and acknowledgement of the Haitian support in gaining their independence. This small country is special despite the negative images and propaganda that is promoted of it. I knew I would return back in a different capacity and be part of something. It was an experience I would never forget.

Presenting and participating at an Educational Symposium

When I returned back to the United States, I was driven, excited, and ready to finish my studies. I shared my adventures with my family and friends. One friend in particular always listened attentively to my description of her land, country, and culture.

She helped me tremendously with my creole and later became "madanm mwen" (my wife).

Fast forward, I graduated from CUNY Brooklyn College with my B.S. in Health and Nutritional Science and a minor in Education.

Haitian Proverb:

Konn li pa di léspri pou sa

Knowing how to read does not mean you
are smart

(The level of education of a person is not a proof of
intelligence)

3

TEACHING

"Dr. Jean-Paul, a service leader, the word "impossible" is not in his vocabulary. His commitment to building an authentic professional relationship with students starts with knowing their names, and takes the form of recognizing students as they pass through the hallway." - Dr. Selma K. Bartholomew "Dr. B.", President of Partner With Legacy (DBA)

At this juncture of my life, I was working for a non-for-profit company and doing substitute teaching. In the evening, I would volunteer at a local church and mentor students. After a year, I took a Science teaching position at Satellite Academy High School. This is one of the oldest alternative High School in the nation. The school was created for over-aged under-credited youth. Many of the students faced tough obstacles while attending a traditional High School and needed a change in environment. I was responsible for teaching them content and preparing them to pass the New York State Regents Examination/Performance Based Assessments. In addition, I was an advisor for a small group of students in ensuring that they stay on track for graduation. I was their father, uncle, guidance counselor, teacher, and mentor. I admired all the students who came to the school. Their resilience and determination to complete High School was admirable.

We must accept that traditional learning is not for everyone and can be challenging. A creative approach to learning is always needed for schools. Social-Emotional development and balancing learning are always required for our students. As a teacher, I loved the classroom, the questions, discussion, and challenges that young people bring into the classroom. The creativity and art in developing a lesson plan are fun. If you have a good relationship with your students, they are willing to sit back, lean in, and learn. I always assessed my students to check for understanding. I appreciated their feedback and honesty. This allowed me to grow as an educator. I am still learning.

One practice I incorporated in my toolbox and took with me as an administrator is the use of protocols. The use of protocols helps drive instruction and promotes critical thinking. For example, when I would discuss various NY Times articles, the students would select the type of protocol to use to discuss the topic. The discussions would get so deep that I would have to write late passes for students to get to their next class. In group discussions, I would have a note-taker, time-keeper, questioner, etc. Each group would share, out loud, their learnings.

My bulletin boards would show the celebration of student work projects across the classroom. The board would consist of the following: a title, the task, rubric, my name and course name, student and actionable next steps to increase student outcomes. I was mindful of saying, "good job" or "nice intro" because the board does not explicitly tell the student what is being celebrated and excludes opportunities for further growth. This reminded me of my responsibility to always set high expectations for my students and community.

I was a teacher but also an advisor. I had a group of 16-20 students that I was assigned to. My family group or advisor group was fun. We discussed various topics from sports, inequities, race, money management, economics, stress management, college and career options, etc. I would push my group to think and ask them to explain and cite evidence. We were a meaningful group and every voice was heard. As educators, we have a responsibility to talk with our students and help them navigate through tough times. The teaching staff was supportive and collaborative. They helped me understand the complexities of culturally responsive teaching. The conversations and modeling were effective. I am forever thankful for what I learned as a teacher and student.

When I became an assistant principal, I was extremely nervous, but also happy and excited. I decided to leave and start a new high school. I embarked on a journey supporting the new school leader, teachers, and students. Replicating what you do in the classroom is different now, however still possible. I helped create a culture and implemented practices that supported the school's success. The first goal was establishing trust and helping my staff understand the data that tells us about our students.

After that first year, I had grown tremendously. Finding a balance was a challenge at first. I would hold a benchmark with teachers and coaches to discuss goals progress. I would support them with current state standards and the school's mission. The communication was ongoing and transparent via verbal, email, and scheduled conferences. The goal was always tied to improving student learning outcomes, lesson planning with best strategies, students' data, and action research. In addition, I would provide teachers with information on relevant workshops offered by the school district. The team/department meetings shared best practices and resources. We had many celebrations for all teachers.

The school environment was safe, clean and respectful and the halls were dressed with students' work. We were a college preparatory High School and determined to make sure every student applied to the college or university of their choice. Students start visiting colleges in the 9th grade and afterwards. We had to make sure to encourage every student to believe in themselves and follow through with their commitment. The administration, teachers, and community applied for various programs and implemented them in the school. We had some challenges but were able to show progress. I love the responsibility the entire staff took to ensure that post-secondary planning was in effect for the students.

Over the years, my leadership skills had improved vastly. I learned to unite teachers under the vision of my school leader. I am especially proud of the culture that grew over the years. The evidence accumulated over the years in students' work, teachers' observations, and learning narratives. My steps grew deeper in the work and I was happy and proud to have helped establish the groundwork. The staff went deeper in their interpretation of how to use the data and made purposeful changes in their curriculum.

One of my darkest moments as a teacher at that time was when I lost a student due to gun violence. I was on my way to work when I heard on the radio that a young lady was shot and killed. She was a bystander when two people were arguing on the streets in Upper Manhattan. I immediately called my supervisor and he informed me that I would have to take the lead in dealing with this crisis as he was recovering from an illness. When I arrived at the building, I immediately met with the staff and we designated a space on the 4th floor as a memorial for the student. Students left messages and paintings for her. In addition, we set up counseling spaces for students to cope with this senseless loss.

During my tenure as a teacher, I took on many leadership roles. My superintendent selected me to enter a graduate program to obtain my Masters in School Administration and Supervision. I was encouraged by my colleagues and mentors. At the time, I was already enrolled in a Master's program for teaching but made the switch to school administration.

My mentors were Dorothy Joseph and Denise Cummings. Ms. Joseph authored a book entitled "The Tale of Two Systems". She was a passionate teacher and educator for many years. Ms. Cummings was also a great teacher and administrator with the department of education for many years. She helped many international students obtain teaching certification and support. I saw my grandmother in both of them. They both reminded me of my role in education and responsibility as a man of color in leadership. They warned me of the future failures, successes, and limited opportunities I would encounter. However, they told me never to lose hope and reminded me that this path was chosen for me.

Haitian Proverb:

Bay piti pa chich

To give little is not that we are stingy

(It's not because we give little that we are necessarily stingy
or that we have bad intentions)

4

LEADERSHIP

"Leadership is a call to service. Dr. Max Jean Paul has been answering that call from the moment I met him at Satellite Academy High School"
- Ingrid Roberts-Haynes, New York City Department of Education

After several years as a teacher, I decided to help a colleague, Derek A. Jones, start a new High School. He heard about my work ethic and passion for education. I am very thankful to him and the team for giving me the opportunity to create a wonderful High School. We conducted many presentations, meetings, and town halls with community members. The school was approved by the Department of Education and was placed in a large comprehensive building. The facility could hold four thousand students.

In NYC, many large comprehensive High Schools were phased out to create smaller learning communities (Horace's Compromise). The purpose of this model was to improve graduation rates and help reduce the dropout rates. In the building, shared facilities remained the same, like a cafeteria, gymnasiums, and auditorium. As the assistant principal, I was responsible for instruction, organization, and climate.

The next step after the approval would be the recruitment of students and staff. Parents had to get to know us, believe in us, and trust us with their children for the next four years of their lives. The school was placed in a building that had low graduation rates, attendance rates and perceived as dangerous. Their children's safety was in our hands. We created a college/university onboarding culture and supportive environment for our students. The student population was great and the parental involvement and community engagement was also high. After four years, each of our students were accepted into college. After the first year of the school opening, other small schools opened in the building with different themes, but all focused on students getting into the college or university of their choice.

One memorable moment was taking the juniors on a Civil Rights Movement thirteen day tour. The tour began with us landing in New Orleans and conducting some habitat work in the ninth ward. This was post-Hurricane Katrina. We visited Mississippi, Arkansas, Alabama, and Tennessee. The students met with civil rights leaders such as

James Meredith and Elizabeth Eckford. Mr. Meredith was the first African-American to attend the University of Mississippi. He spoke with the students about his struggle in dealing with racism and how he stayed focused. Ms. Eckford was part of the Little Rock 9, the first group of African Americans to integrate into the school post Brown vs. Board of Education. Both of their stories brought chills to my spirit and had a tremendous impact on some of the students. It was an honor to meet these icons of the civil rights movement.

We also visited key historical sites where sit-ins took place and where meetings took place. The tears and joys after each visit were priceless. All of the museums were filled with artifacts and history of the civil rights movement. The students walked across the Selma Pettus Bridge in Selma, Alabama and sang a "Freedom Song". Our trip concluded in Atlanta, Georgia. The students shared the impact of the trip with the school community and did small projects honoring our nation's civil rights movement.

Dark Moment

On January 12, 2010, I received a frantic phone call about an earthquake in Haiti and it was all over the news. The earthquake had a magnitude of 7.0 and many aftershocks afterwards. Many buildings and monuments were destroyed. Over 100,000 thousand people died. I was concerned about the students and families that were impacted, not knowing if their loved ones were okay back home. The following day, I met with the staff when I arrived and we reviewed our plan of action. We conducted town hall meetings with students and had a safe space for them to talk to our counselors. It was a busy week.

A couple of years ago, I attended a ten-year anniversary since the inception of the new school. It was overwhelming and an honor to see former students as teachers, lawyers, and doctors. Overall, the school building was transformed into a dynamic learning complex. The community was happy with the transformation and I was delighted to be part of that success.

During my tenure as an assistant principal, I was nominated a couple of times to pursue the principalship by senior leadership. I declined many times due to family obligations and personal reasons. I enjoyed my role as an assistant principal. I loved working with teachers on creating a culturally relative curriculum and seeing it executed in the classroom. I enjoyed engaging with students in classroom discussions and clubs. While representing the school and speaking at community events as a leader, I would take part in other conversations about race and culture, local and state mandates, perceptions, and social dilemmas.

Conversations

There is a clear distinction that people of color in leadership have to deal with than other ethnicities. There is a sense of responsibility, understanding, perception, stigma, barriers, resistance, and baggage that leaders of color must face. I refer to this as the "lack of equity in the room." The race challenges in the districts were not present. The cultural differences were missing. I was the black male with dreadlocks representing a small high school in a room with large comprehensive High School leaders led by other races. The issue of systemic racism disguises itself in many settings. I would have to experience this once a month during school district meetings. School district resources vary in New York City-based on zip codes. (Meatto, K 2019)

The small talk with other colleagues would be brief, and I would move forward with taking notes and returning back to my school with relative information. The self-awareness and reflection continued to push me in my leadership role. Our students' performance in examinations and college acceptance helped leverage the conversations around data, system-wide plans, and cultural influences.

Leveraging conversations

The principal and I would set time to discuss these matters. It was important for us to share our experiences in our cabinet meetings and address the concerns to move the school successfully. Isolation and loneliness are normal in leadership (Emdin, C. 2016), but it does not have to be like that all the time. We continued to lead the school with excellence and provided a great learning environment. As a leader, it is important to be persistent and keep the students in mind. The distractions, mandates, systemic pillars, and obstacles can be overwhelming. However, I learned the importance of having a plan each day, follow up on small tasks and what is not done today can be deferred for tomorrow. I am thankful to the courageous leaders in education who address black males, black leadership, women, and its impact on public education. Some of their suggestions and advice were beneficial in my growth as a leader. Following their example, I took the baton and began to speak and write more about some of these disparities in public education. If I wanted students who look like me to have more access, it was important for me to be their constant advocate.

I begin to explore and interview for a principalship. I had a choice between schools and decided to take over an alternative high school, to be more specific, a transfer High School and night program for older students. Being a transfer school teacher, I understood the challenges, creativity, and passion in working with this population. In addition, the resiliency that students bring in wanting to earn a High School diploma and post-secondary options.

The school was scheduled to close due to low graduation rates, low regents' rate, and dropout rates. I laid out a clear plan and vision to turn it around with the support of the teachers, community, and stakeholders. The next chapter outlines the school, structures and systems that were put in place. I am very proud of the work and gains the school has made since I took over. Our literacy program, social justice approach, and graduates are special. Our motto is "Building Bridges for Tomorrow," which was created by our staff. My current students realize it is their "last chance" to succeed. I have created a learning environment to address life issues that may impede academic success. My students are provided with access to job-readiness programs, training, subsidized internships, college trips, counseling and case management.

Haitian Proverb:

Sa foumi genyen, se sa'l bay pitit li

What an ant has, it's what she will give to
her child

(A mother gives what she can to her child)

5

PRINCIPAL

In 2010, I took over Brooklyn Bridge Academy High School. BBA is an alternative high school in NYC serving students who are over-aged and under-credited. On any given day during class transitions, you can sing along to the classics, rock, hip-hop, rap, and jazz. Bob Marley said that "One good thing about music when it hits you feel no pain." The love of music is common ground between adults and children, but when children come to school, they are expected not to have access to the music they and their teachers love.

At BBA, we are determined to build solid relationships and rapport between the adults and students. Therefore, we continue think out-of-the-box. During class transition, we play songs that are chosen and loved by students, teachers, community-based staff, and administrators.

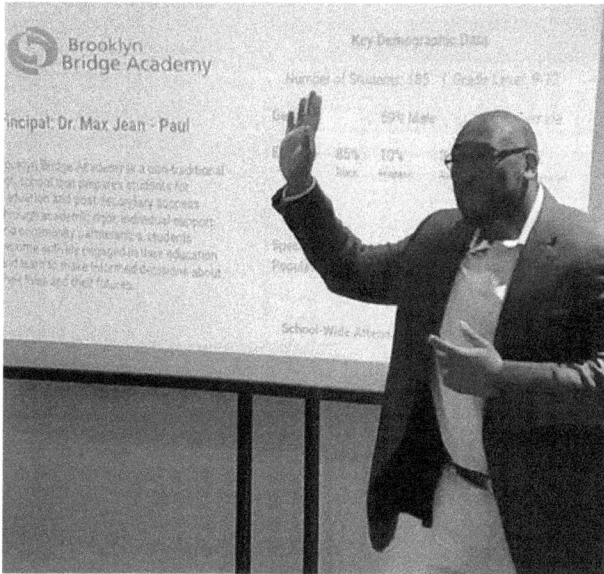

Presenting at a National Educational Conference.

About BBA:
Looking beyond the demographics

Brooklyn Bridge Academy (BBA) is a small New York City Alternative high school that currently serves over 75% of Title I learners. We know and understand that the statistics limit the deeper understanding of who our students are and the promise of what BBA, as an alternative high school, offers our students, their families and future generations. The tapestry of our students' lives reflects various cultural and linguistic backgrounds representing communities that include African Americans, West Indians, South Americans, and African Immigrants. We serve students who are, in reality, still children. However, life has demanded that they grow up quickly.

Brooklyn Bridge Academy's model embraces a vision of college and career readiness. We believe that every student is a unique learner whose interests and passions we seek to spark and enhance to enrich classroom and positive school experiences. Our students benefit and persevere from strong partnerships with the teacher, leaders, and all school community members who consider the academic and social success of our learners as their central mission.

The personal challenges our young high school-aged students face, derive from social disorganization which are often reflected in their dispositions. For our young men this includes age, color, defensiveness, frustrations, vocal and non-verbal demands to never be disrespected. And then at times, our young men are extremely playful. They love sports and talking about their favorite team and playoff hopefuls; music is an integral part of who they are, how they define themselves, and when they meet their friends, they want to give and receive "dap or pound". The disposition of our female students is similar in that they demand to be respected; they have a difficult time letting go of confrontation and may be perceived at times as unforgiving. However, our young women have to learn to be high school students which is reflected in how they dress, the wearing of a trendy knock-off bag, their excitement to participate in school trips and their sincere happiness when they learn that they will get to participate in school prom.

At BBA, we provide a safe space and an education bridge for students who, as result of social disorganization, may be living in shelters, foster homes, young parents, children struggling to maintain family ties at home, trying to exit the juvenile justice system, students who struggle not to become a victim of the sex-trade industry that preys on young women in urban communities, students who are parents themselves and trying to re-define their relationship with their parents and at the same time define their role as a young father or mother. We also serve young women who may be pregnant or young men expecting to be a young father. In addition, we assist students who, along with their parents, are newcomers to the country. We keep in mind that we also have students who have been separated from their parents for years as their parents worked to establish citizenship in this country and now being re-united as teenagers with their parents without having had any psychological support to deal with the feelings of abandonment that may be unspoken in their relationship. We also keep in mind that we serve students who have a traditional family structure— yes, both parents are in the home, yet are struggling with how to communicate with and manage a teenager who feels the impacts of social disorganization.

As a transfer school, BBA is committed to ensuring that our learning culture and climate actively address social disorganization with 3Rs: Relationship, Rigor, and Readiness.

Social Disorganization

The theory of social disorganization is not widely known in education. It is therefore not factored in when discussing schooling and the needs of our children who in reality are facing seen and unseen dangers that arise from social disorganization throughout their lives. The theory of social disorganization was developed by sociologists, Shaw and McKay (1942), who were seeking to analyze and explain violence within communities. The idea of social disorganization looks closely at how communities are organized or disorganized, which significantly impacts the lives of the community members. Specifically, in education, there is a great deal of deficit and blame game thinking that serves to dishearten our leaders and educators. Disheartening because the current discourse from the climate of NCLB (No Child Left Behind) looks at schools through a lens of failing rather than asking how the purpose of a school within a community serves to address social disorganization factors that significantly impact educational outcomes.

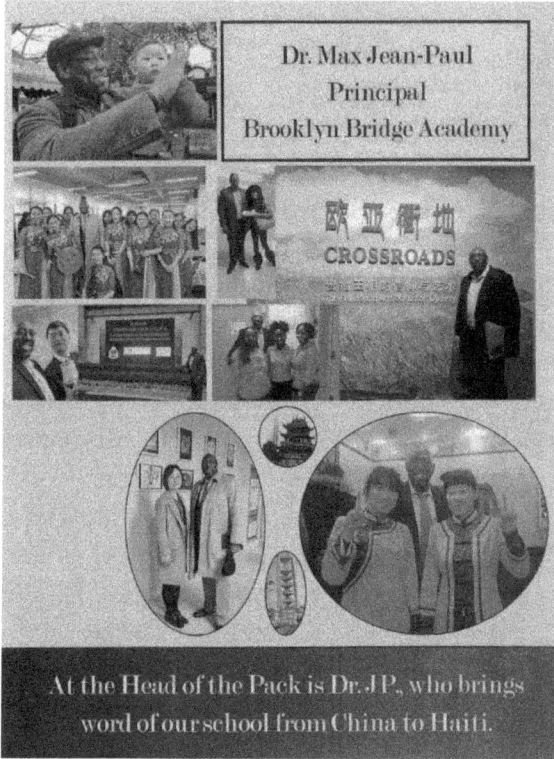

Dr. Max Jean-Paul
Principal
Brooklyn Bridge Academy

欧亚衢地
CROSSROADS

At the Head of the Pack is Dr. JP., who brings word of our school from China to Haiti.

If we take a close look at most of the education research done today, we discover that far too much research is being done on a child's demographics because that is easy to categorize, rather than considering the community as a whole. Specifically, there are so many studies done on single-parent households and educational outcomes rather than examining a community and the impact of single-parent households on schooling. According to Na'im H. Madyun (2011) " If the research is not focused enough on social explanations as opposed to an overemphasis on individual and/or classroom – level factors." There are many factors that affect students' chances of obtaining a High School diploma. Exposure to positive and uplifting reinforcement makes a big difference. Madyun notes that "A potentially unseen danger in past research on African –American achievement has been focusing too narrowly on poverty as a condition or reality and not as a structural limit to potential socializing opportunities".

Our BBA students often feel overwhelmed, ashamed, and uncertain because they know that they have failed to complete high school requirements on time and at the same time with their childhood friends. Despite their dispositions and social challenges, we know and believe that educators have to offer students hope with meaningful relationships and educational models that will help them to complete high school and transition to college and career.

BBA's model has served to graduate over 1000 students. The staff reflects on those efforts and hopes in sharing our model, what worked, obstacles faced and what we envision as some of our next steps. This document also reflects a dialogue and a desire on the parts of the authors to generate a more inspiring discourse on how to meet the needs of our children. They who are on the fringes of education as a result of social disorganization rather than the current model which seems to rate public schools as failing rather than places to grow and inspire hope.

We wanted to break away from deficit thinking and offer a working and continuously evolving model for public high schools, such as BBA, who are serving some of our most needy children and families. We want others to know that what we do in public education matters to each student, their families, and community.

Relationships

As a school, we have been proactive about the role of the new federal standards. To reach it, we understood the value of relationships among stakeholders. In our school, getting new students any day during the school year is a part of the norm. Every time a new student is introduced into the environment, we are open to the unsettling discourse for the new student, their peers, and their teachers. Why is it so unsettling for members of the community? For a student who has recently been incarcerated and entering back into a community school setting or for a student who has not had successful relationships with adults, trust does not come easy. Teachers, who have the pressure of the test, to meet the demands of federal standards, struggle with managing new students with tough dispositions, orientating them to classroom norms and yet still being creative. Teachers often feel derailed in their daily norms.

Given the emotional challenges our students face outside of school, we know that trust is difficult for our students, which is why we are committed to building relationships with our learners. Relationships can only be cultivated with strong working systems and structures that are constantly examined and refined.

Breakfast and snacks are available all day. Teachers understand why we needed to do this. The paradigm of schooling is determined by traditional views and ingrained mental models about what schooling and the activities of schooling should look like, feel like and sound like. In most schools, food remains in the cafeteria and is only served early morning.

We discovered that the negative disposition is often a result of our young men and women coming to school hungry. Mom or Dad may leave for work early morning or they may be in a stressful foster home setting. We also have to openly admit that some of our students are dealing with substance abuse issues. As a result, they are often unable to say "I am hungry," and before we instituted all day breakfast, students were irritable or lethargic and struggled with keeping focus.

Teacher Teams Fuel Relationship Building

To create a culture where our teachers are constantly asking the question of who our students are, we committed to developing teacher teams as the engines of our school. Teacher teams are responsible and accountable for our students' academic, social, and emotional development and for setting professional expectations for each other. Our teams are organized by content and also the needs of the students. We have had to do some out-of-the-box thinking and approaches to help our teachers better know our students and develop meaningful relationships with them if we are to get them to re-engage in learning. For example, we organized our teachers into small sub-groups and tasked them with getting to know our students and implementing an activity that would bring teachers and students together in a fun way. At first, this was a challenge for the adults because it meant figuring out what they liked to do, but also letting go of the old and getting to know their students who are often guarded. The outcome was that the teachers accepted the challenge and took the risk and organized Zumba classes, cooking classes, chess games, and they discovered that our girls, and yes some boys, wanted to learn how to crochet.

Ambivalent relationships are present in all organizations, including schools. Therefore the structure of common planning supports teacher collaboration which serves to foster professional relationships. As a principal, it is important to know that developing a shared vision takes time and a commitment to protecting structures and systems that serve to allow teachers the time to establish a working professional relationship as teams. At BBA, teams meet 2 to 3 times per week during the school day to look at student work, assess student progress, and plan the next steps for students and student sub-groups. They conduct curriculum to share guidance meetings, and descriptive reviews of students. The teams develop goals and implement common strategies to promote student achievement. Teams are constantly asked to reflect on the progress they are making and how their students will know that they are a team.

Our teams also receive technical support from instructional coaches to help them develop and refine action plans and deepen their content and pedagogical practices.

Learning is ongoing and facilitated with professional readings and study which serve to guide our practices. We have had professional discourse using some of these resources

- Addressing the Attitude Gap (Kafele. B. 2013)
- Growing Roses in Concrete (Dr. Jeff Duncan-Andrade)

For the past 5years, we have been engaged in lesson study to get teachers to provide critical feedback and evaluate what is working. Our lesson study implementation has included the following:

- Teachers meet during common planning to unpack literature and professional readings on lesson study
- Teachers meet to identify the lesson and plan the lesson collaboratively
- Teachers identify students who will be closely observed during the lesson to assess the impact of teaching
- Teachers debrief what they observed within teams and the whole staff

- Teachers reflect with colleagues on practices and identify next steps for the teacher and also next steps for future lesson study.

Principals Must Be Willing to Walk the Fire

One of the systems and structure that make us unique as an NYC high school is our commitment to having a Community Based Organization (CBO) that is integrated into our school model.

A positive working relationship with your CBO is essential to success. Principals must be willing to walk through the political fire to identify and partner with a CBO who will form norms, and storm with them to execute their mission of serving high needs students. BBA's original design and model included a Community Based Organization as partners. As we reflected on our eight-year journey and changes that we made to the partners who were at the table with us, we have found that the greatest obstacle is ensuring that the CBO is keenly aware of and understands the families we serve and their needs and conditions. In addition, we have also learned that the CBO must be well organized in its approach to forming relationships with the teaching staff, students, and the school community.

We currently partner with CAMBA which utilizes a Primary Person Model. Providing adults assigned to each student who understand and take ownership of their responsibility for establishing a rapport and relationship with the student and their family. The advisors' primary function is to determine what the needs of the student are and what obstacles they are facing that may get in the way of their academics. They must be aware of what challenges arise from serving students from diverse cultural backgrounds. For example, relationships matter if we want undocumented parents to open up to us, trust us, and tell us what specific support they need; work, housing, and health care. CBOs provide an ongoing needs assessment of our students as it relates to housing policies and needs, immigration policies and obstacles, translation services, maneuvering the judicial system, accessing homeless services and other community based programs. They also assist in finding ways to help our students and their families overcome hurdles that range from accessing substance abuse programs, health care services, and even navigating the system to save their homes from foreclosure.

The CBO must also be strong partners in providing learning to work coordination that purposefully connects students with internships, allowing them to form valued relationships with mentors who provide encouragement and insights on what to expect in the work world.

Rigor

Within our learning culture we define Rigor as Reach. We want our teachers to understand the design and implement lessons with tasks that demonstrate a reach for all learners. We work to actively create an "excuse-free" learning zone where staff, faculty and students are accountable for results. This means that staff must clearly and coherently define high expectations that engage and inspire students to be active learners in their own human potential. We openly admit and do not shy away from the fact that the work level must take into account the prior knowledge of our learners, assessment targets, and our goals for equipping our students to be prepared for college and a career. Over-aged and under-credited youth often feel disempowered by their previous educational experiences.

At BBA, we continue to place heavy emphasis on both long and short-term goals. We know that our students have academic challenges, so we provide a customized approach. Students are provided an academic program that is supported through tutoring, extended day, and Saturday Academy. Additionally, our students are required to meet with their advisor once every two weeks to assess progress and performance. Students cannot remain anonymous within our educational space which prevents students from falling through the cracks. Both teachers and advisors work with students to set goals and realistic benchmarks. The challenge is that because our students are dealing with so many personal challenges, they may share private information with an advisor that they are not ready to share with a teacher, so ensuring that students feel safe and supported is a balance that we must always be aware off. We proactively utilize structures and systems to ensure that teachers and advisors are on the same page and aware of what is happening academically and emotionally with students.

Students set goals for graduation and credit attainment. Our approach to credit attainment is non-traditional. Our school operates on a trimester that includes cycles and BARs. First, the academic year is broken up into a trimester to allow students to object to accelerated credits. Each trimester is referred to as a cycle where students are taught content and skills for Regents based courses and we implement BAR biweekly assessments.

The Biweekly Assessment Reports (BARs) show the students' progress during each 10-day grading period as well as the average of all preceding grading periods. We meet during Wednesday advisory pullout in which each teacher is assigned to a small group of students with whom they meet once a week to review BARs and set goals for the next BAR period, the cycle and beyond. Advisors utilize dictation to identify individuals and groups of students for targeted intervention. This practice continues to highlight the collaboration between advisors, teachers, and students and places the ownership for goal setting on the student while providing both emotional and academic support.

College pathways include college advisors who work with students to identify two or four-year colleges and universities. Students and parents receive support through the entire process from college visits, completing the application, and transition out of high school. Ongoing parent outreach focused on awareness and engagement of school curriculum, learning goals and accessing resources to assist both students and their families.

Our Learning Culture and Expectations

Students will develop the skills of using evidence to support arguments in discussion, which will then transfer to stronger writing, literacy, math and develop the communication and collaboration skills that support college and career readiness.

Students will respond to quick writes. The use of quick writes is a practice that we continue to build on so that we are not only improving regents' scores to passing, but we are preparing our students for college.

Students will engage in high-quality discussions, exemplified by responding to and extending each other's thinking and crafting questions to help each other deepen and elaborate upon their thinking. Teachers will use question stems in order to facilitate high levels of discussions.

Students will become independent in developing higher-level questions for the purpose of academic discussion across BBA classrooms.

In addition, two years ago, we implemented BOOK END, a school-wide literacy initiative developed and led by the ELA department in which the school community is engaged in 10 minutes of silent independent reading. This was an opportunity to engage new students because it meant empowering them with choice and also letting them know that if they forgot their book at home that day, the rules were not going to change—they had to work with their class teacher to find a book in class to read. When we first implemented this structure, we had to engage in the professional discourse to ensure that all our staff understood our data and why reading time for students in school was critical to creating a learning culture. We first tried to do this at the end of the school day. However, it didn't work because the end of the day conflicted with other school activities and we needed the full buy-in of teachers and students. We didn't abandon this strategy, instead, we examined the structure and made adjustments. We now implement for 10minutes before lunch.

Book End looks like, sounds like and feels like:

- All members of the community engaged with reading
- Classroom libraries reflecting the interests of students and the goals of teachers
- Level books available
- Students and adults talking about their favorite read and characters
- Students embracing a new author and feel accomplished knowing that they completed a book that they wanted to read

Readiness

Brooklyn Bridge Academy is a school focused on re-engaging high school learners as they work to meet NYS standards, regents goals and prepare for work life, college, career, and beyond. Ensuring that students are prepared with the academic and life skills aligned to NYS learning standards is essential across all departments. Our core value is that the child's social emotional component must be addressed prior to addressing academic skills. This collaboration is essential in developing the school model, instructional framework and leads to college and post-secondary readiness. We continue to move forward by aligning our understanding of the student focused instructional practice. Teachers use various strategies to address readiness and learning styles in a student-centered environment, First we implemented foundation classes in English, Math, and Science that are designed for new students entering BBA. Specifically, science teachers, in collaboration with coaches, examined regents goals and college readiness goals in science and made a decision about key scientific thinking skills that needed to be developed to help our students succeed in Living Environment, Science Ethics, and other science courses. In our foundation classes, students developed a fundamental understanding of what is an inquiry in science, how to reason and conjecture, how to write a well-developed lab report, explore their understanding using quick writes, how to take risks and write, research using credible sources and develop the academic vocabulary needed to support their learning in higher level courses. Students are taught skills in preparation for regents based courses. This is evident in the increased rates of students passing the regents exam.

Our learning culture includes

- Dedicated advisors provided by CAMBA
- Our learning environment which presents college information
- Speaker forums
- College Trip
- Parent Workshops

At BBA, we continue to expose our students to promising careers and new outlooks in life. We want students to feel and understand success. What does it mean to make it? What does it mean to build a bridge for tomorrow? We collect our resources to help students journey through High School and obtain a college acceptance letter. This is done by academic interventions and quarterly community gatherings. Finally, parental involvement also aids in helping our students overcome many obstacles.

BBA continues to embrace a vision of college and career readiness for our students that is anchored in the belief that every student is a unique learner whose interest and passions we seek to spark and enhance through an enriching classroom and positive school experiences. Our students benefit and persevere from strong partnerships with teachers, leaders, and all school community members who consider the academic success of our learners as their central mission. We are committed to shaping students' academic skills, drawing on their personal resilience and increasing their academic performance. The goals of ensuring that students are prepared with the academic and life skills that are aligned to federal standards are essential across all academic departments

Overall, we believe daily reading builds stamina and fluency. Strong readers make for better, more enlightened citizens who learn how to navigate the world. We believe literacy is central and essential to our lives as students and as human beings. We continue to work with families to emphasize the importance of attendance to facilitate higher academic achievement. With the assistance of CAMBA personnel and New Visions, we continue to plan and make clear the link between attendance and the academic process. I appreciate these organizations' values in democratic reforms and public education.

Haitian Proverb:

Kréyol palé, kréyol konprann

Creole spoken is creole understood

(Speak plainly, don't try to deceive)

6

LESSONS LEARNED

Dealing with outside forces
Political Issues and Leadership

Black Lives Matter

As a black man growing up in the United States of America, the issue of race is a political matter. As mentioned earlier in the book, I was aware of who I am at a young age. My family provided me with some of the tools to navigate systemic racism in the United States of America. The readings, conversations, images, implicit bias, and imprisonments of innocent people over the years helped me deal with this burden each day. James Baldwin says, "Not everything that is faced can be changed. But nothing can be changed until it is faced."

The senseless killing of Trayvon Martin hurt me. It could have been my son, student, relative, or me. I understood the fear that my students experience when they leave their homes and encounter law enforcement.

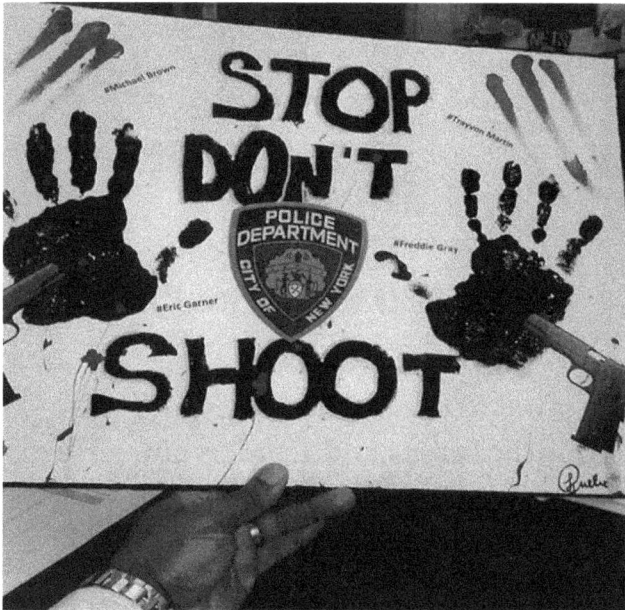

Prior to that, Kalief Browder was in jail for allegedly stealing a backpack. Reading about his story and witnessing these events continued to divide our nation. I tell my students, "Your blackness should not be your obstacle".

These incidents in America do not go away. It reminds me of the two systems in our country that benefit others. As a leader, I was aware but needed to speak up about it. We held multiple town hall meetings in the school to improve police relationships. Students voiced their struggles and provided solutions to improve communication. The partnership with law enforcement became stronger.

We dedicated one of our yearbooks to the Black Lives Matter movement. My staff understood that any of our students or relatives could have been victims of these senseless acts. We developed curricula and asked reflective questions to help our students cope with these tensions in the United States. I am very proud of the work we continue to do at our school to help raise awareness and deal with race matters and their implications on our youth.

Food Distribution with community members

Understanding my students' goals, needs, and interests in returning back to school was important for me. It was important to meet them at their level and create a plan. The baggage for students varied after each semester. However, it is our goal to make sure that they achieve success.

Besides food and shelter, students need to have a connection with the school. My years of education have taught me that it comes down to relationships. Relationships help in classroom instruction, applying to college, and waking up every morning to come to school. Students believe that someone is there for them. As a leader, I continue to model that for my staff.

I remember my first year at the school. The school color was orange, so I painted all the doors orange over the weekend. Students were amazed and expressed their gratitude for the change. Their voice helped drive future projects, trips, and events at the school.

After many years, I still enjoy being a principal. To see some of my students come back to visit the school is priceless. They are engineers, carpenters, plumbers, and teachers. Some of them have started their own families and businesses. I am proud of each and every one of them.

Challenges

As previously mentioned, when I took over the school, I was informed that the school could close. I was very upset and disappointed because I had just arrived. However, I presented my three-year plan to turnaround the school to the State and City officials. In addition, I advocated for the need for a school like mine and how disrespectful it was to suggest that the school be closed. Parents and representatives from the city and state understood my concerns. As a result, I was given some time to make changes and the school started to make yearly gains. With the support of teachers, New Visions for Public Schools, instructional coaches, and the community, we successfully moved from a dismal rating of "C" to an "A".

A few years later, the department of education wanted to reduce the number of classrooms and relocate the school to another section in the building due to a charter school coming into the complex. Because we were an alternative school, I felt that the central office was treating the school and students as if they did not matter. The staff, students, and I protested against the move. I spoke at various meetings and asked parents and graduates to petition against this move. We ended up losing three classrooms but maintained our space in the building. It still saddens me that we had to go through that process. I remember one student asking me, "JP, what happens if we lose?" I expressed to him that I would do everything possible to fight for our school.

As a leader, I continue to advocate for my students to succeed. They come from various backgrounds, genders, and challenges. I teach them to create their narratives and have a voice in making their decisions. I recall two students from Jamaica. They were placed in the wrong grade when they arrived in the United States. They were not doing well and transferred to my school. I asked them if they were motivated and what they wanted to do in three years. They wanted to graduate from High School and become engineers. I told them we would make a plan and I will sign their High School Diploma. After one year, they graduated and went to college. They came back 2 years later to thank me and the staff for our assistance. I expressed to them that it was their determination and passion that we supported in helping them to succeed.

Another student who climbed his own mountain at my school was from Haiti. He was limited in English but was determined to graduate from High School. He lost his mother, failed the NYS regents exam but he did not quit and completed his High School requirements in two years and went onto college. These are the stories you do not forget.

Each of these stories and many more represent the lives of students that have passed through the BBA hallways. The multiple conversations, tears, hopes, and determination are what make the school special. The teachers and support staff that lend both hands to support our young people is important. Most of the students have hardship problems and never had the opportunity. With motivation and high expectations, they succeeded.

Hope

On Thursday, January 11th 2018, on the eve of the 8th anniversary of the Earthquake that devastated Haiti, I received a frantic call from a relative about President Trump's comments about Haiti and African nations. She said, "Mwen Sézi", meaning I am shocked. I was angry and started to develop a headache. As a father, and school leader, what was I going to tell my children and students? One of my students came to me and said, "Dr. Jean-Paul, Haiti does not get a break, but we will be alright". I replied, "The people are resilient, despite the obstacles the country faces".

Haiti is a beautiful country. The mountain ranges, rich culture, and delicious food are incomparable. The people welcome you with open arms and are always willing and eager to provide assistance. If you get lost, someone will help you narrow your way to your destination.

Unfortunately, natural disasters, political softball, and other issues continue to impact the country. After the Earthquake in 2010 and recently Hurricane Matthew (2016), many Haitians had to relocate to the United States. I was fortunate to organize a Hurricane Matthew relief effort with a team of educators and other schools to deliver supplies and professional development materials for students and teachers. Thank you, Harold Simeon, Principal Claubentz Dieujuste, and everyone who joined forces to help bring sustainable aid. The voices of the students' struggles rose above the crumbling surroundings and multiple challenges they faced. Listening to their tales about the strong winds and fallen trees from Hurricane Matthew was scary. However, they remained resilient and came to school.

A year later, teachers and students began having conversations around teaching and learning, curriculum innovations and challenges. The benefit of future international exchange began. We cultivated a relationship among students and faculty in understanding other countries' educational systems.

The current negative remarks and actions toward the nation and its people are unacceptable and heartbreaking. There is no justification to understand the President's remarks. It is simply wrong.

As a leader, I will continue to salute and share my heritage and encourage all the Haitian diaspora to remain hopeful.

Celebrations

It is an honor to be a principal and a voice for my students. They come from various backgrounds and tough neighborhoods. My staff and I have provided a positive learning environment for them that provides motivation and promise.

Several students and I, in partnership with another school, visited Tokyo, Japan. Students were excited and appreciated the experience. When we landed at Narita International Airport, the students could not believe they were in Japan. The smiles on their face were priceless.

I reminded them that you could be whatever you want despite gender or race, and look at what you are able to accomplish at a young age.

Educational expedition to Tokyo, Japan

I emphasized having the right mindset and staying focused on their task . We visited many museums, Mount Fuji, and experienced taking the bullet train.

Students shared their experiences with the school community and were able to understand the differences between the cultures.

Mount Fiji, Japan

In 2019, I was invited to be part of a small delegation of school leaders to attend a trip to the People's Republic of China. We had to take a few classes at the China Institute and Confucius training to learn about Chinese culture and tradition. The workshops provided a foundation of the learning institutions we were going to visit and an understanding of the educational system in China.

A monument in China

While I took workshops, my school community created small tokens of quotes and inspiration for me to present to my new partnerships with the People's Republic of China. They were very thankful and open to hearing more about schools like mine. Every day, I sent pictures and videos of my trip to share with my school community. The pictures and videos were screened on the two LCD screens in my school hallways. I remember my custodian and students saying, "I finally get to see China in real-time". In China, I was brought back to my childhood memory of having a scheduled menu. I knew I was going to have rice as an option to eat. People would look at me with curiosity due to the color of my skin. I took multiple pictures of Shanghai's skyscrapers to the beautiful red lights of Beijing and festival boats on the Huangpu river. Our first visit was to East China Normal University. The professor and students provided an overview of the Chinese educational system. The presentation was through the lens of daily student life in China and tracks taken after state examinations. I was impressed with the value of daily eye exercises and physical education. Our other visits to schools and institutions were very productive. The representatives wanted to hear and learn from the US delegation.

Art exhibit in China

This helped promote further relationships and some schools in our network have sent students to study abroad in the past years. Finally, I appreciated walking the great wall of China. The feeling was a little similar to the second time I climbed the Citadelle LaFerrière due to the historical relevance of borders. The mountains and scenery are beautiful.

One of many school graduations

I have created an "excuse-free" learning zone where staff, faculty and students are all accountable for our results. My students work very hard to achieve what they did not think they were capable of. This is why they deserve a wonderful learning experience.

Haitian Proverb:

Prémyé so pa so

The first fall is not a fall

(A missed first try does not really count, you have to roll up
your sleeves and try again.)

7

CONCLUSION

Thanks to my culture, grandparents, parents, and family, I believe in empathy and understanding. Leadership always requires courage and building the people around you. Knowledge is meant to be shared. I clearly and coherently define high academic expectations to engage and inspire each student to be active learners invested in their own human potential. I also remind them to always show gratitude and appreciation.

I continue to work with my staff to implement the best instructional strategies in the classroom. We share ideas, lessons, and experiences to look for ways to grow. The student work and assessment data help us in making decisions for our students. While being a principal, I have spoken at many speaking engagements on leadership, equity in schools, the role of black males, teaching, learning, and mentorship.

Projects in Haiti

I continue to work in Haiti as a volunteer educational consultant. I helped create the Society of Haitian School Administrators. As president, we conducted a one-day Educational Summit in Leogane, Haiti with the support of over twenty organizations abroad and local. The organization goal is to promote global practices for aspiring administrators, promote equity, and 21st century leadership skills for all.

Educators from Haiti attended this free summit with workshops and received a certificate from a US college for participation.

The Society For Haitian School Administrators Educational Summit

Haitian Proverb:

Piti, piti, Waco fè nich li

Little by little the bird builds its nest

(With time everything is possible)

ACKNOWLEDGMENTS

I want to first acknowledge and thank my Supreme Being for giving me life and helping me each day. Thanks to everyone around me who encouraged me to write. Thanks, Melissa, Jickael, Maxberte, Papy, and Selma for your patience and contributions.

Thanks to everyone who has had an impact on my life. From the streets of Brooklyn, to my Haitian household here and abroad, close friends and mentors who have come into my life. It was not easy at times and thanks for providing me with the guidance and steps to move forward. You are not forgotten Thank you.

To my children, remember to stay strong and support each other. You inspire me. Both of you are kings and remember to move forward in life. Create your own narrative. You are seen and heard. You will have problems but take the time out to find a solution. You can do this. Your mother and I are very fortunate to have both of you. Be brave, resilient, and kenbé la!! Live your lives with purpose and passion.

As I share in my weekly column, Message to the Youth, when challenges come, stay positive. Embrace challenges as a learning experience and remain focused. You are in charge of your own destiny.

MOUNTAINS

ABOUT

MAX R JEAN-PAUL Ed.D.

Max R. Jean-Paul, Ed.D. is an educator and international consultant on school reform. He has advised school districts, universities, and educational organizations on numerous issues, such as race, at-risk youth, discipline, and safety. Over the last decade, he has lead a transfer High School. A graduate of Fordham University, he has authored numerous articles and has served as the President of the Society for Haitian School Administrators.

He travels to Haiti and remains deeply committed to the work of changing lives and mindset through engaging professional learning opportunities. He works with school leaders in NYC and internationally to help inform best practices to ensure that children who have traditionally been marginalized are provided with competitive advantages in school and community.

Follow on Instagram: @EmpowermentThroughEducation
Follow on Twitter: @DrJean_Paul
Email: dr.mjeanpaul@gmail.com
Leadership Development Opportunity

"Dr. Max Jean Paul is one of the premier thought leaders of our time. In his book, he walks us through the mountains he had to climb to overcome challenges and how he is using his life experiences to empower today's scholars." - Jeff Lindor, Founder of The Gentlemen's Factory Inc.

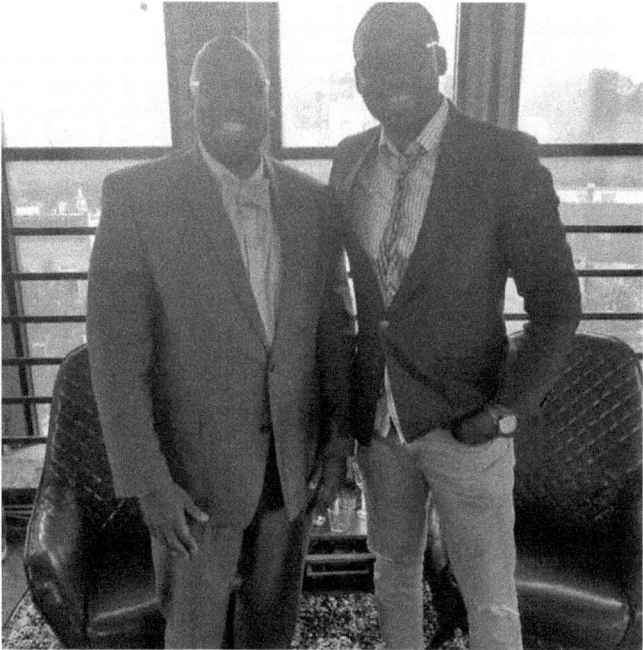

Myself and Jeff Lindor, Founder of The Gentlemen's Factory Inc

The Bridge Multicultural & Advocacy Project Event

Male Empowerment Event (Dress for Success)

Food Drive for Brooklyn Shelter

"FINI"

BIBLIOGRAPHY

Barth, R.S. (1990). Improving schools from within. San Francisco: Jossey-Bass

Baldwin, J. (2017). I am not your negro. Vintage Books.

Cushman, K. (2003). Fires in the bathroom: Advice for teachers from high school students. New York: The New Press.

Darling-Hammond. L (2010). The flat world and education. New York: Teachers College Press.

Deal. T.E., & Peterson, K.D. (1999) Shaping school culture: The heart of leadership. San Francisco Jossey-Bass.

Delpit, L. (2006). Other people's children: Cultural conflict in the classroom. New York: The New Press.

Emdin, C. (2016) For the White Folks Who Teach in the Hood and the Rest of Y'all Too. Boston, MA. Beacon Press

Fullan, M. (2014). The Principal Three Keys to Maximizing Impact. San Francisco, CA. Jossey-Bass.

Gassaway, B. (2006). Reflections of an Urban High School Principal. Jamaica, NY. Gassaway ALG.

Hammond, Z. (2015). Culturally Responsive Teaching & the Brain. Thousand Oaks, CA: Corwin Press.

Howard, G. (2006). We can't teach what we don't know. New York: Teachers College Press.

Heifetz, R.A. & Linsky, M. (2002). Leadership on the Line. Boston, MA. Harvard Business School Press.

Henderson, N. & Milstein, M.M. (2003). Resliency in

Schools: Making it Happen for Students and Educators: Thousand Oaks, CA. Corwin Press.

Kafele, B. (2009). Motivating black males to achieve in school and life. Alexandria, VA: ASCD.

Kafele, B. (2013). Closing the Attitude Gap. Alexandria, VA: ASCD.

Lemov, D. (2010). Teach like a champion:49 techniques that put students on the path to college. San Francisco: Jossey-Bass

Madyun, N. H. (2011). Connecting social disorganization theory to African American outcomes to explain the achievement gap. Journal of Educational Foundations, 25, 21-35.

Moss. M. C. & Brookhart. S.M. (2012). Learning Targets Helping Students Aim for Understanding in Today's Lesson. Alexandria, VA: ASCD.

Oluo, I. (2019). So You Want to Talk about Race. New York, NY. Hachette Book Group.

Shaw, C. R. and H.D. McKay. (1942). Juvenile delinquency and urban areas; A study of rates of delinquents in relation to differential characteristics of local communities in American cities. Chicago: University of Chicago Press.

Singleton, G.E., & Linton, C.W. (2006). Courageous conversations about race. Thousand Oaks, CA: Corwin Press.

Sizer, T. (2004). Horace's Compromise: The Dilemma of the American High School (0 ed.). Mariner Books.

Stepick, Alex; Stepick, Carol Dutton; Eugene, Emmanuel; Teed, Deborah & Labissiere, Yves (2001). Shifting identities and intergenerational conflict: Growing up Haitian in Miami. In Ruben G. Rumbaut & Alejandro Portes (Eds.), Ethnicities: Children of immigrants in America (pp.229-266). Berkeley, CA: University of California Press.

Tatum, A.W. (2009). Reading for their life:Building the textual lineages of African American adolescent males. Portsmouth, NH: Heinemann.

Trilling B. & Fadel C. (2009). 21 Century Skills. San Francisco: Jossey-Bass

https://www.history.com/this-day-in-history/haitian-independence-proclaimed

https://www.history.com/topics/1980s/just-say-no

https://www.nytimes.com/1990/03/08/nyregion/boy-13-arrested-in-burning-of-11-year-old.html

https://www.nytimes.com/1989/08/25/nyregion/black-youth-is-killed-by-whites-brooklyn-attack-is-called-racial.html

https://www.nytimes.com/2019/05/02/learning/lesson-plans/still-separate-still-unequal-teaching-about-school-segregation-and-educational-inequality.html

https://www.history.com/topics/1980s/central-park-five

https://www.britannica.com/place/La-Citadelle-Laferriere

https://www.npr.org/sections/pictureshow/2020/01/12/794939899/haiti-in-ruins-a-look-back-at-the-2010-earthquake

https://www.britannica.com/biography/James-Meredith

https://www.nytimes.com/2019/05/02/learning/lesson-plans/still-separate-still-unequal-teaching-about-school-segregation-and-educational-inequality.html

https://www.youtube.com/watch?v=GB8mTOiQXjY

https://www.britannica.com/event/shooting-of-Trayvon-Martin

https://www.schoolreforminitiative.org/protocols/

https://www.nytimes.com/1986/02/02/nyregion/fha-case-recalls-bushwick-in-70-s.html

https://www.schoolreforminitiative.org

https://www2.ed.gov/nclb/landing.jhtml

https://www.youtube.com/watch?v=2CwS60ykM8s

https://www.edweek.org/teaching-learning/opinion-using-japanese-lesson-study-to-increase-collaboration-among-teachers/2016/04

www.ingramcontent.com/pod-product-compliance
Lightning Source LLC
LaVergne TN
LVHW011336080426
835513LV00006B/383